D1737315

21st Century Skills Library

CITIZENS AND THEIR GOVERNMENT

# LOCAL ACTION

*Frank Muschal*

Cherry Lake Publishing
Ann Arbor, Michigan

Published in the United States of America by Cherry Lake Publishing
Ann Arbor, MI
www.cherrylakepublishing.com

Library of Congress Cataloging-in-Publication Data
Muschal, Frank.
 Local action / by Frank Muschal.
   p. cm.—(Citizens and their governments)
 ISBN-13: 978-1-60279-061-2
 ISBN-10: 1-60279-061-2
 1. Municipal government—United States--Juvenile literature. I. Title.
II. Series.
 JS331.M87 2008
 320.8'50973—dc22                                    2007006765

*Cherry Lake Publishing would like to acknowledge the work of*
*The Partnership for 21st Century Skills.*
*Please visit www.21stcenturyskills.org for more information.*

# TABLE OF CONTENTS

# CHAPTER ONE

# GOVERNMENT IN THE UNITED STATES

*The federal government is the same for all citizens, whether they live in Alabama, Alaska, Wyoming, Vermont, or any other state.*

You are an American. As a citizen of the United States of America, you

have certain rights and privileges. The federal government is responsible

for looking after many of those rights and privileges for you.

The federal government protects Americans from foreign invaders. It makes treaties with foreign governments and declares war when that is necessary. The federal government prints the money, runs the national parks, and controls the Army, Navy, and other military forces.

*No matter when you read this book, hundreds of thousands*
*of other Americans will be serving in the U.S.*
*military on that day to protect you.*

*States can be large like California or small like Delaware, but they all have basically the same duties to their citizens.*

Besides being an American, you are the resident of one of the fifty

United States. You might be a Texan, Alaskan, Minnesotan, or New Yorker.

You might live in a state with many other people, such as

California, or in a state with relatively few people, such as New Mexico.

State governments cannot declare war or print money. They have other responsibilities to their residents.

State governments make rules for the businesses that operate within their borders. They issue licenses for activities such as driving cars, hunting, fishing, cutting hair, and operating restaurants—and state officials check to be sure that these licenses are up to date and their provisions are being followed. State governments set laws for people who live there, such as the speed limits on many roads.

Learning & Innovation Skills

State laws cannot cancel out federal ones. How does this keep the country running smoothly?

**Learning & Innovation Skills**

Why is it useful for the three levels of government to share some powers and responsibilities?

Within the state where you live, local areas are divided into sections called **counties.** Inside the counties are cities and towns. Counties, cities, and towns have their own powers and responsibilities to make sure that people can live and work together. These are all local governments, and they are concerned with the problems people face on a daily basis. They make sure that garbage is collected, that clean water flows into homes, and that people are kept safe from crime.

All three levels of government—local, state, and

federal—share some responsibilities and powers.

These include collecting taxes, maintaining roads,

writing and enforcing laws, and spending money for

the public good.

Citizens, however, have only two main

responsibilities: they must obey the laws, and they

must pay taxes. Citizens have one great power,

too. They can vote. Voting is both a right and a

responsibility in a democracy such as ours.

Americans need to improve their voting record! In recent elections, voter turnout was just 45 percent of eligible voters. In comparison, for the same period, voter turnout in Brazil was 76 percent. In Canada, it was 60 percent, and Italy had a dazzling 90 percent turnout.

Voting is important. It is how we elect the people who make the laws and who keep our governments running smoothly. Americans vote to make sure that government meets our needs.

In a democracy, government is expected to follow the will of the people. It is difficult, however, for single individuals to affect national government policies. It is also not easy for one person to affect state government policies. However, individuals can influence local issues in a big way!

# CHAPTER TWO.

# How City Governments Work

*City councils, such as this one in Asheville, North Carolina,
meet regularly to conduct town business.*

City governments are usually led by an elected mayor or by a city

manager, who is hired by the city council. City council members

themselves are elected by the residents of the city that they serve. Large

cities may also be divided into districts or wards with a council member for each district. Just like the federal and state governments, city governments represent the voters who elect them.

A city council meets on a regular schedule to do the town's business, and the meetings must usually be open to the public. Council members vote on the city's annual budget. The council considers applications from people who want to do business with the city. They review zoning appeals from people who want to open a business in one neighborhood or to stop a business from opening in another neighborhood.

Within a city's government, there are departments that handle the everyday functions of the city. The fire, police, and sanitation departments are the most visible. Larger cities often have many other departments such as planning and development, tourism, and human services.

City residents who have an issue that needs to be resolved can usually contact the department that is concerned with that issue. For example, if residents notice gang activity in their neighborhood, they can ask the police department to increase patrols in the area. For example, Chicago's Department of Streets and Sanitation has a program called Graffiti Blasters.

When someone paints graffiti on a wall, neighborhood residents call the Graffiti Blasters, and a team arrives within two or three days to remove the scrawl. Taggers get discouraged when their hard work disappears so quickly. Graffiti in Chicago has decreased significantly.

However, existing departments sometimes can't deal effectively with an issue. That is when citizens must bring the issue to the attention of the city council.

*Dealing with the damage caused by graffiti is*
*a major focus of many city governments.*

# CHAPTER THREE

# LOCAL GOVERNMENTS MAKE NEIGHBORHOODS SAFER

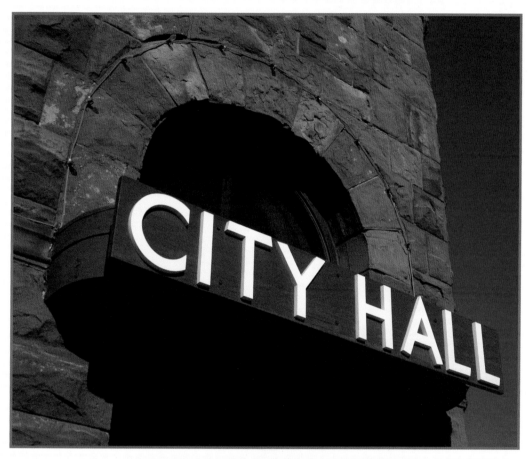

*Many towns hold their city council meetings in City Hall, which may also be the central police station, jail, and mayor's office.*

Let's visit a typical city council meeting to find out how things work.

To do this, let's go to the town of Austin, Iowa. The city council held a

*Making street crossings safer is one topic for city council meetings across the nation.*

regular meeting on April 13, 2007. **Minutes** from the previous meeting were read and approved. Old business was brought up. Some of the old business was discussed and completed. Some old business needed more investigation and was rescheduled for the next city council meeting. Then new business was called for.

Sitting in the audience was town resident

Noah Lucas. He was concerned about a dangerous

intersection in his neighborhood. Mr. Lucas had

asked Councilwoman Kim Milligan to sponsor a

motion to install a stop sign at the intersection.

Councilwoman Milligan investigated the intersection

herself and asked local residents their opinions.

Most were in favor of a stop sign. Ms. Milligan

took pictures of the traffic and wrote down the

names of local businesses and the locations of

nearby playgrounds.

Many people find working in local government very rewarding. What are some of the key skills and knowledge you need for such jobs?

Councilman Krouse rose to give his opinion. "I was almost run over at that very intersection. The volume of traffic on 3rd Avenue has increased a great deal since that new subdivision went up nearby."

Councilman Perry suggested that a more scientific study should be done to measure the volume of vehicles and pedestrians at the corner. Mayor Brayman asked if money was available to put up the stop signs. The town's Director of Finance said money was available.

Mayor Brayman suggested that a traffic study could be **waived** to ensure that the intersection be made safe as quickly as possible. Some discussion

*City council meetings, such as this one in Asbury Park, New Jersey,
are often covered by local TV and newspaper reporters.*

followed. Then Mayor Brayman called for a vote. The motion was passed.

Mayor Brayman said that his office would begin the process for installing

the stop signs the next day.

Noah Lucas took on the responsibility of making a dangerous intersection safe for his children and for the other children in the neighborhood. In doing so, he showed leadership in his community. Think of a problem in your neighborhood or town that you would like to see addressed by your local government. What facts would you present to the city council to make your case?

Noah Lucas saw a problem in his neighborhood, and he spoke with his council member about it. Councilwoman Milligan investigated Mr. Lucas's claim and saw that the intersection was becoming dangerous. She brought the issue up before the city council, and steps were taken to correct the situation. This is an example of how a citizen can influence local government on behalf of public safety.

# CHAPTER FOUR

# LOCAL GOVERNMENTS HELP
# LOCAL BUSINESSES

*Providing suitable parking facilities can be a big problem*
*for huge cities as well as small towns.*

Later that evening, Councilman Canton presented a petition submitted

by storeowners near the town train station. The petition said that

commuters were parking their cars for free in front of the stores close to

the train station instead of paying for parking in the train station lot. The

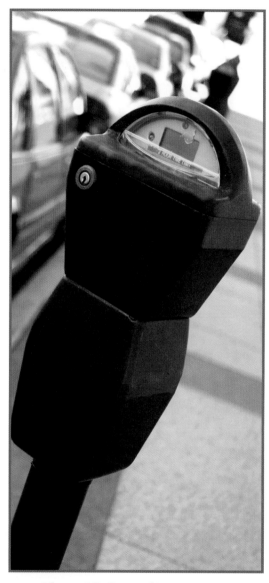

*The world's first parking meter was installed in Oklahoma City, Oklahoma, in 1935. Since then, millions more have been installed in the United States and elsewhere.*

businesses claimed that because the cars were parked all day, many townspeople were doing their shopping in the mall outside of town rather than in the downtown stores.

Councilman Caton suggested that installing parking meters would encourage commuters to use the designated lot and free up the parking spaces in front of the stores for shoppers. He made a motion to study the feasibility of installing parking meters along the streets near the train station. The motion was seconded and passed.

The mayor requested that various council members and city administrators look into different parts of the issue. Councilman Caton agreed to meet with downtown storeowners to determine how many parking meters they thought should be installed. Mayor Brayman asked the head of the Department of Finance to look into the costs of various types of meters and how much and how long installation would take. The mayor also said that he would speak with the mayor of nearby Bedford Falls to see if the recent installation of parking meters in that town

**Learning & Innovation Skills**

Do you think it is the responsibility of a town's council to help local merchants conduct their business? Why do you think that way? Hint: Think what your community would be like if some of your favorite business moved away.

was helping their downtown businesses. Everyone agreed to report his or her findings at the next council meeting.

When old business was called for at the next council meeting, the parking meters were brought up for discussion. The Director of Finance said that installing more than 200 parking meters would put a heavy financial strain on the city budget. Councilman Caton said that about 280 meters were needed to protect all of the stores near the train station.

Then Mayor Brayman explained what he learned about the situation in Bedford Falls. The new parking meters there were generating revenue that was helping to defray the cost of installing them. More importantly, the businesses in Bedford Falls were making more money because nearby parking spaces were now available to their customers. In addition, Bedford Falls itself was taking in more money from the sales taxes that customers paid. The mayor of Bedford Falls had projected that the parking meters would pay for themselves in three years. After some discussion, the motion to install 280 parking meters in downtown Austin was passed.

When the meters were installed in the downtown area in Austin, local commuters soon began to park their cars in the designated train station lot,

**Learning & Innovation Skills**

Traffic and parking are a major issue for many cities and towns. While some are putting in parking meters and garages, others are banning vehicles completely. What would you do to make sure people had convenient access to businesses — without constant traffic jams?

where all-day parking was available at a reasonable rate. Local downtown businesses were very pleased. They had been able to get the city council to take action that benefited their businesses and, in the end, had helped the town as well.

*Getting the right mix of human and car traffic is critical to the economic success of business areas around the world.*

# CHAPTER FIVE

# TO SERVE THE COMMUNITY

*Council meetings in large cities can involve hundreds of people.*

In some very large cities, being a city council member is a full-time

job. There are many more people to represent, and large cities are more

complicated to manage.

In smaller towns with smaller budgets, council members often receive

only a token payment for their services. Council members might be

**Learning & Innovation Skills**

Watching and listening to a council meeting can be very interesting. Find out when your town has its next council meeting. Make plans to observe it with some friends to see how the council operates.

teachers, retirees, or merchants. Whatever way they make their living, they all have one thing in common. They want to make their community a good place to live. What else does it take to be a city council member?

Different towns and cities have different qualifications for city council members. Many qualifications are similar, however. For example, towns may require that council members be registered voters and have lived in the city for a specified length of time. To be a voter, means that candidates for office must be at least 18 years old. Some cities require candidates to be 21. Sometimes candidates need to supply a petition with signatures

28

of a certain number of people who want them to

be council members. Often candidates must pay a

fee to run, too.

Running for local office takes time and money.

Serving as a city council member usually pays very

little. It takes special people to give their time to the

community. It takes people who understand that

one person can make a difference. Perhaps it is not

so easy to change the world, but every one of us

can make our neighborhoods better places to live.

If everyone did one thing to make our hometowns

good places to live, imagine how wonderful life could

be for us all!

21st Century Content

What might be some issues that modern-day city council members might have to deal with that people in the past would not have? Hint: Think about modern technology, such as cable TV and cell phones, and present-day health issues, such as bird flu and mad cow disease.

# GLOSSARY

**city council (SIT-ee KOUN-suhl)** group of elected officials who conduct the business of a city or town

**city manager (SIT-ee MAN-i-jer)** professional leader hired to direct the operation of a city or town

**counties (KOUN-tees)** largest political divisions of land within a state for the purpose of government

**democracy (di-MOK-ruh-see)** type of government in the United States in which citizens vote on a regular basis to elect people to lead them

**feasibility (fee-zuh-BIL-uh-tee)** ability to be accomplished

**mayor (MEY-er)** elected leader of a city or town

**minutes (MIH-nuhts)** written summary of a formal meeting

**motion (MOH-shuhn)** formal proposal brought before a legislative body

**petition (puh-TISH-uhn)** written request signed by many people asking that a certain action be taken

**voting (VOHT-eng)** process in which citizens chose their leaders

**waived (weyvd)** put aside or not enforced

**zoning (ZOHN-eng)** legal mechanism for local governments to maintain and control the distribution of housing, businesses, factories, and other establishments within the city limits

# FOR MORE INFORMATION:

## Books

Giesecke, Ernestine. *Local Government.* Chicago: Heinemann, 2000.

Russell, Kenneth, and Margaret Russell, *"How" in Parliamentary Procedure.* Danville, IL: Interstate Publishers, 1999.

Silate, Jennifer. *Your Mayor: Local Government in Action.* New York: Rosen Publishing Group, 2003.

Tames, Richard. *A Young Citizen's Guide to Local Government.* London: Hodder Wayland, 2001.

## Other Media

*American Government for Children–Federal, State and Local Government.* VHS. Schlessinger Media, 2005.

For links to Websites on city, town and county governments and much more, go to *http://www.usa.gov*

For the official Web portal to local government information, go to *http://www.firstgov.gov*

# INDEX

## ABOUT THE AUTHOR

**Frank Muschal** lives in Chicago with his elderly cat, Agatha. ("She's older than laptops and cell phones, but I'm older than TV.") He's been writing and editing for textbook publishers for thirty years and has no guilt feelings about tormenting students all that time. Besides writing, Frank keeps busy playing tennis, riding horses, and fumbling around on his guitar. "I'm no rock star," he says. "I just want to make me more interesting to myself."